IN
YOUR
SOUL

Let the divine words of God's truth pierce your heart.

TRUST HIM

By Kristine Gabriella

Trilogy Christian Publishers

A Wholly Owned Subsidiary of Trinity Broadcasting Network

2442 Michelle Drive

Tustin, CA 92780

For information, address Trilogy Christian Publishing

Rights Department, 2442 Michelle Drive, Tustin, CA 92780.

Trilogy Christian Publishing/ TBN and colophon are trademarks of Trinity Broadcasting Network.

For information about special discounts for bulk purchases, please contact Trilogy Christian Publishing.

10 9 8 7 6 5 4 3 2 1

Library of Congress Cataloging-in-Publication Data is available.

ISBN 979-8-89333-036-6

ISBN 979-8-89333-037-3 (ebook)

IN

YOUR

SOUL

Let the Word of God pierce your heart.

TRUST HIM

By Kristine Gabriella

DEDICATION

To my God, who has never left me and has walked alongside me through everything in my life, even when I was not paying attention to Him. Praise for His grace, the beauty of His love, and for all the times of heartache and disappointment. Thank You for never giving up on me even when I did not trust You.

To my two most amazing, caring, and thoughtful sons, Scotty, and Cody—you are the loves of my life. Thank you for your never-ending love and support. You both have shown me how to love myself and how to trust God in even the most challenging times. Loving you as a Christian mother has been my biggest reward in life. I am truly thankful for your hearts for God. You both inspire me to be a better person.

To my beautiful daughters-in-law, Amanda and Samantha. Thank you for always supporting me, listening to me, and loving me so well. Thank you for continuing and encouraging our Christian faith in our family. You are a blessing to my heart.

To my precious grandchildren, Mia, Millie, and Vincent, my heart overflows with love for you. You fill our family with so much joy, happiness, love, and laughter. We are so blessed to have you. I hope KK will always be an inspiration to you to be strong, brave, and reach for God in everything you do in life.

To anyone who reads this devotional, my hope for you is peace and contentment in knowing God will always be by your side and work everything out for good. Trust Him. I pray for God's words of truth to pierce the very depths of your soul.

Blessings always, Kristine.

PREFACE

From a loving son,

The heart of this book and Kristine's journey is "trust Him completely." The author, my mother, has greatly exemplified this motto throughout the highs and lows of life on this earthly realm. As an adult now, I've watched her trust God with everything, and I mean everything. Even when at times my anxious inner voice would suggest, "Well maybe don't trust Him with that," she stayed the noble course in full faith. Parenting? Trust Him. Finances? Trust Him. Cancer diagnosis? Trust Him. Divorce? Trust Him. Relationships? Trust Him. Choices? Trust Him. Blessings? Trust Him.

The words you will soon read are those empowered by the Holy Spirit. My Mother felt this calling on her heart, so she embarked on this journey to pen a book that challenges us as individuals to trust Him. A lot of us claim we trust God, but when it gets down to the nitty gritty will we? Here is your chance to dive deep into your soul and start trusting Him with a brave heart. Today is Day One of a new mindset. Today is Day One of a new trust. Today is Day One of His will and not your own. This is a brave step you take towards a better self and a step towards Jesus. I pray this devotional finds its true potential and empowers you to trust Him more daily.

Guide me in your truth and teach me, for you are God my savior, And my hope is in you all day long. (Psalm 25:5)

With love,
Scott Anthony Jr.

The Lord directs the steps of the godly.
He delights in every detail of their lives.

Psalm 37:23

⌣

God truly wants to be in every part of your life. He revels in it. He just wants you to invite Him in. How much easier would your life be if you just trusted Him and let Him guide your every step? Life would be so much better. Knowing that He cares that much about you and where you go in life can put you in a state of thankfulness for Him. He is all-sufficient to every one of our needs. Delight yourself in the Lord and His ways. Trust Him and wait patiently. The blessing of the Lord lasts forever. This scripture encourages us to be still and listen to God and His instruction. He will never lead you astray. Everywhere He guides you is for your good and comes from His love. Let Him lead.

In your soul…listen to God's guidance.

For the mountains may move and the hills disappear,
but even then, my faithful love for you will remain.
My covenant of blessing will never be broken," says the Lord,
who has mercy on you.

Isaiah 54:10

———

This scripture is about God's unconditional love for us. Do you accept this love from Him? Do you believe He loves you unconditionally without any question? There is nothing you can do to earn this love. He freely gives it to us because we are His precious children. God's word says no weapon formed against us will ever prosper. Not only does God love us but He will never leave us. He shows constant kindness, grants us His peace, and shows us His mercy. God says the mountains around you may shake to pieces and the hills may disappear. But I will never stop loving you. God's love for us is unfailing. Even at times when God is angry with us, His love is abundant and everlasting. His grace is sufficient, always. The power of God's unconditional love will transform your life. You are worthy and you are loved.

In your soul...embrace God's love for you.

*The Lord is close to all who call on him, yes,
to all who call on him in truth.*

Psalm 145:18

———

Are there times when you do not feel like God hears you? Are there times when you feel like God is so far away from you that how could He possibly hear you? Rest assured that the Lord is always near to the ones who call out to Him. "Call on Him" even when it feels like He can't hear you or you think He is not listening. Believe me, He is always there, and He is always listening to you. Call upon Him, cry out to Him! Praise God for His goodness and faithfulness.

In your soul...cry to Him.

My victory and honor come from God alone.
He is my refuge, a rock where no enemy can reach me.

Psalm 62:7

———

The definition of success is the achievement of desired visions and goals. Success can also be a person with a certain social status because of wealth or popularity. The world says success is attaining wealth, prosperity, and/or fame. Who we are, what we become in life, and what we have already accomplished is only by the hands of God. We must honor Him during our successes because without His blessings we are nothing. We cannot secure the safety of our future without His protection. Against all things. Stand tall. Look to Him. Place your life in His hands. He deserves all the glory and honor, forever.

In your soul...praise Him for His protection.

The Lord is good, a strong refuge when trouble comes.
He stays close to those who trust him.

Nahum 1:7

God is our strength in challenging times. Those who trust God will be provided with His safety and refuge. I remember as a young girl, as soon as it started to rain my brothers and sisters would get so excited. We would hurry and get our bathing suits on, run outside, and find every puddle we could to jump in. What joy our hearts felt as we played in the rain. Then, here it would come, lightning and thunder! Our fun was ruined; we would run to our house. Our front porch became our shelter from the storm. We felt safe. God shelters us from harm. Our only hope is found in His refuge. The meaning of refuge is a condition of being safe or sheltered from the pursuit of danger or trouble. God is protective of His people and His character. He will protect those who put their trust in Him. He is slow to anger but great at protecting His children. *You* are God's child. You are loved and cherished. Take refuge in God. Those who trust in Him must also remember that Christ won the victory at the cross.

In your soul...take refuge with God.

And this same God who takes care of me will supply all your needs from his glorious riches, which have been given to us in Christ Jesus.

Philippians 4:19

⁓

Our God is overflowing with gracious mercy and abundant with lovingkindness. His promises are real and not just words that sound good. He genuinely wants us to depend on Him for everything. As a young girl, I remember my mom running around our house every morning to get all five of us kids ready for school...Yes, five of us! I do not know how she ever did it, but she did it graciously and calmly. We always had our clothes laid out, breakfast ready, lunches made with our milk money sitting next to them, backpacks, and off to school. In all the crazy chaos we always had everything we ever needed to get to school. This is how God is with us. He wants to bless us. He knows our daily needs before we ever ask. God knows that the more we trust Him to supply our needs (not wants), the stronger our faith becomes and the more we grow closer to Him spiritually.

In your soul...rest in Him.

The Lord is my strength and shield.
I trust Him with all my heart.
He helps me, and my heart is filled with joy.
I burst out in songs of thanksgiving.

Psalm 28:7

— ‿ —

Have you ever been out somewhere or driving in your car when your very favorite song of all time comes on? You immediately start belting out the lyrics very loudly, not caring how you sound or what other people think of you. This is exactly how God wants us to praise Him. No inhibitions or thoughts of how we may look or sound. Total openness. Raw. The Lord is our strength. He fills our hearts with joy and song. There is something very edifying and encouraging when we glorify God in the richness of His grace. Singing praise to Him when faced with pain and problems lifts our hearts and gives hope to our souls. Reach out to God in song and praise. Trust Him in your helplessness and give glory to our Father in heaven, for He is good.

In your soul...sing a song of praise.

*It is better to take refuge in the Lord
than to trust in people.*

Psalm 118:8

⁓

Throughout the word of God, we often discover that fearing God triumphs over all other fears or failures. A trusting faith in God gives us a certainty of trust. The fear of man and what He can do to us is a dangerous trap of dread. We are all susceptible to this fall of man; none of us are exempt. Have you ever trusted someone with your life? Truly trusted them with everything within you. And then something happens within your relationship with that person and all trust is broken. Never to be reconciled. Have you ever shared your most delicate thoughts and feelings with this person and found out they shared every detail with your entire friend circle? Only to be humiliated, ridiculed, and judged. This person has become an enemy and not a safe place for you to fall. Was there ever any true refuge or safe place in that person or friendship? We will have trials and tribulations in this life. The Lord Jesus assures us that He has overcome this world and gives us a promise that His grace is sufficient in everything we go through. Nothing will and can ever separate us from His protection, grace, and love. In His power, we can stand firm in the strong armor of God against those who seek to harm or destroy us.

In your soul...have no fear.

*Dear friends, do not believe everyone who claims
to speak by the Spirit.
You must test them to see if the spirit they have
comes from God.
For there are many false prophets in the world.*

I John 4:1

⌣

Are you one of those people who believes everything everyone says is true? Even some of the most farfetched stories? Then, as time goes by their words become less than anything close to the truth. Be careful who you put your trust in. God gives us the gift of discernment through the holy spirit who lives in us. It is also known as our gut instinct. Listen to it. Do not doubt yourself. You are made in God's image. Do not be afraid to trust the spirit for we can overcome the powers of darkness and walk with boldness in this life. Fix your focus on God, His ability, protection, and love. He will do immeasurably more than you can ever imagine.

In your soul...listen to the holy spirit.

Whom have I in heaven but you?
I desire you more than anything on earth.

Psalm 73:25

———

Are you trying to "keep up with the Joneses?" Do you aspire to have the biggest house on the block, the most expensive cars in the driveway, the biggest boat with all the bells and whistles, or the biggest bank account? What are you trying to prove and to whom? That you are better than anyone else? These things are called idols. Worshipping things keeps us from God and His blessings. There is nothing on this earth that is worth desiring more than God alone. Idolizing things is the way of the world. Are you in the world or of the world? As Christians, we should only be in the world not of it. As followers of Jesus, we cannot be both because eventually, one will take over our lives. Such behavior can lead us to isolation from God and His word. Do all these "things" mean more to you than God? Think about that question. Isolation from God then leads to our destruction, including a spiritual battle. Let your desires be only for God, the almighty prince of peace. Allow God to be the strength in your heart and your portion for eternity.

In your soul...set your desires on Him.

Do not love money; be satisfied with what you have.
For God has said, "I will never fail you.
I will never abandon you."

Hebrews 13:5

————

Remember when you were little, and the tooth fairy (your parents) would give you money for losing your teeth? Or when you would get dollars in your birthday cards. My grandpa Vernon Wright would line up all of us grandkids, eight to be exact, in single file and hand each one of us a dollar bill. You would have thought He handed us a 100-dollar bill. He would then get out His stash of candy that He surprisingly kept in the freezer and let us all take whatever we wanted. He made us feel so rich. My eyes would always get so big, and my heart would jump, with a smile so big it covered my entire face. It was so exciting to know that when I got home, I would put that dollar in my piggy bank for safekeeping. My next thought was saving up enough money so I could buy the next baby doll I so desperately wanted. Or maybe a new red bike like Becky down the street was riding around. At an early age, money becomes something that we dream of having. It seems to make us happy. As we got older, I remember my dad sitting at the kitchen table every month grumbling over the bills and being short of money. It changed my view on money. I always watched my parents work so hard to provide for our family. It made me sad that money had become a worry, making Him angry and upset. I quickly lost my fascination with money by witnessing the hardships it put on my family. We always managed to have everything we ever needed. That is God taking care of all our needs. In this scripture: it says be satisfied with what you have. Trust Him today for all your needs.

In your soul...remember God will never fail you.

Trust Him

Those who listen to instruction will prosper.
Those who trust the Lord our God will be joyful.

Proverbs 16:20

———

Do you remember the childhood song: "I've got joy, joy, joy, joy, down in my heart, down in my heart, down in my heart? Down in my heart to stay." How can we ever sing these words without feeling such happiness and joy? Wouldn't it be great if we woke up every morning singing this song and embracing these words of joy? Well, you can! The holy spirit is in us and wells up when we are feeling happiness and joy. Let the spirit move your soul. Proverbs 17:22 says "A joyful heart is good medicine, but a crushed spirit dries up the bones." Let the holy spirit flow like water through your heart and let your days be filled with pure joy from God. Always remember to lean on the father and trust in Him.

In your soul...embrace the joy of the holy spirit.

Trust in the Lord and do good.
Then you will live safely in the land and prosper.

Psalm 37:3

———

I surrender all. I surrender all. All to thee My blessed Savior. I surrender all. As a Christian, I say I trust God with everything in my life, but do I? I pray the same prayer repeatedly because that is what worry will do to you. Is this trusting God? I would say no. Worry leads us astray from God's truth. Every week at church I sing from my heart praising and worshipping God for all He does. My heart lays my burdens at the foot of the cross with real meaning and conviction. Then as soon as I walk out the door thoughts start running through my head, and worry creeps in. Why do I make life so difficult for myself? *Stop*. Rest in His goodness. His peace. His comfort. God wants us to trust Him and His will for our lives. Believe Him and your life will prosper more than you can ever imagine.

In your soul...truly surrender all. He will do the rest.

I Praise God for what he has promised.
I trust in God, so why should I be afraid?
What can mere mortals do to me?

Psalm 56:4

———

Remember the old saying, "Sticks and stones may break my bones, but words will never hurt me?" This saying is unequivocally false. We know that words can truly break our hearts. The Bible says: "The tongue has the power of Life and Death and those who love it will eat its fruit." The wrong words can ruin a relationship repeatedly. Words can destroy our motivation and inspiration. What happens in our lives when we continue to carry that bag of sticks and stones that hurt us so deeply? It keeps us from everything good God wants for our lives. Our burdens weigh us down emotionally and spiritually. We are barely able to move forward. We become stuck in our misery caused by someone else. By believing the words of other people, we have allowed them to keep us down. As we work through this process by believing the truth of God's word, we are set free. We get rid of the sticks and stones in our bag, one by one until there are just some small slivers of sticks and tiny pebbles left—remember we are never without some sort of difficulty in this life. Bask in the glory of knowing He is with you every step of the way.

In your soul...praise God for His Word.

We know how much God loves us,
and we have put our trust in his love.

1 John 4:16

———

My dad was a quiet man until He was sitting at the kitchen table every month paying bills. It was during challenging times that He would speak up. He never learned how to share His feelings or thoughts with our family. But all I had to do was look at Him and I saw the love He had for me. It was not until the day I graduated high school that He said "I love you" for the first time I ever remembered in my life. Having Him look at me and say those words made it so special and meant so much, even though I always knew He loved me. Having confidence in God's love comes from knowledge about His love. Truly knowing Him. How do we know God loves us? It is by His constant presence and the way He reveals Himself to us that we can feel His love. Even though He knows every sin we have ever committed, He still seeks after us daily. His grace is sufficient. His love is powerful. His name is Abba Father. God is love and will always be LOVE. There is no fear in His love. He says, "Whoever lives in Love lives in me."

In your soul...feel God's love.

Don't let your hearts be troubled.
Trust in God and trust also in me.

John 14:1

———

As Christians, we often forget that there is a Holy Trinity consisting of God our Father, Jesus Christ our Savior, and the Holy Spirit. God is three persons in one. They are inseparable. All three persons are 100% God. The Father, the Son, and the Holy Spirit are all fully God Himself. Colossians 2:9 says of Christ, "In Him, all the fullness of deity dwells in bodily form." Meaning the being of each person is equal to the whole being of God. The three divine persons are distinct in their own way. We are baptized in their name. They share one essence. They are *one* God. In this verse, Jesus is speaking to us. He is giving us comfort and hopes that He will one day return for us. He exhibits the heart of God to draw us nearby. He encourages us to put our trust and faith in God. To not be troubled with the worries of today. Through Jesus Christ, we can see the glory of God. He is full of grace, truth, and love. Let God hold your heart. Trust Him to take care of your every need. See Him for who He is. The one and only I AM.

In your soul...let your heart rest in the Holy Trinity.

Trust Him

Though a mighty army surrounds me,
my heart will not be afraid.
Even if I am attacked,
I will remain confident.

Psalm 27:3

Have you ever been shopping on Black Friday? It is the quintessential day after Thanksgiving Day. It is traditionally the start of the Christmas shopping season. Many stores offer highly promoted sales at extremely discounted prices to lure customers in. Black Friday, although an exciting time and tradition for many families, can feel like a war zone. It is chaos, with long lines and extreme traffic jams. People will gather in large groups pressed together with no way out, fighting to get every item on their list. Pushing, yelling, shoving, arms flying, and in extreme instances health scares of heart attacks and passing out. For what? Why would anyone put themselves in harm's way? To save a few dollars? In this life, we will experience troubles. It is a promise. But we do not have to worry for in this scripture, God promises protection against all enemies and armies against us. Our hearts can be still and confident, knowing we have faith and trust during uncertainty. No matter what happens God is with us, always. When we walk by faith, we can rest in God's gracious embrace.

In your soul...remain confident.

He will not let you stumble, the one who watches over you will
not slumber.

Psalm 121:3

How many times have you gotten up in the middle of the night to use the restroom or get a drink of water and you tripped over some random object that doesn't even belong on the floor? Stubbing your toe and in excruciating pain wanting to scream out for help but you cannot because everyone else is asleep. We feel helpless and in pain. Sometimes we just want to cry. Just know that when God says He never leaves us, He truly does not. He is our protector day and night. God never sleeps. He will not let us stumble.

In your soul...rest in the truth that God will never let you fall.

Look at the birds. They don't plant, harvest, or store food in barns, for your heavenly Father feeds them. And aren't you far more valuable to Him than them?

Matthew 6:26

———

Do you ever worry about how you will buy groceries this week or if you will have enough food for the 37 guests coming to your house for a going away party? Worrying is unproductive. It does nothing for our lives but causes us unnecessary stress. Jesus tells His followers not to be anxious about food. We must rely on God who fully provides for us. He says you are worth more than the birds in the sky, and they do not go hungry. God calls us to fulfill the purposes of the kingdom if we are distracted with worry, we are unable to do that.

In your soul...trust God to provide.

And my God will meet all your needs according to the riches of His glory in Christ Jesus.

Philippians 4:19

———

God truly has everything we will ever need. Scripture says God will provide all that we need according to *His* riches. He does this by providing all that is best for us, not what we think we need. God knows our daily needs before we even ask. God's perspective of what we need has eternity in view. God also knows that the more we trust Him to fulfill our needs, the stronger our faith becomes and the more we grow spiritually.

In your soul...trust God to know what is best for you.

But blessed are those who trust in the Lord
and have made the Lord their hope and confidence.
They are like trees planted along a riverbank, with roots that
reach deep into the water.
Such trees are not bothered by the heat
or worried by long months of drought.
Their leaves stay green, and they never stop
producing fruit.

Jeremiah 17:7-8

So many times, in life and in different situations, I hear people speak about being blessed. I often wonder how they are blessed. Did God bless them? Did He answer a prayer? When we put our trust, hope, and confidence in God, it gives Him an open door to show us His magnificent blessings of peace and joy. Stay firmly rooted in His truth and your worries will wither away.

In your soul...trust His blessings.

Fear of man will prove to be a snare, but whoever trusts in the Lord is kept safe.

Proverbs 29:25

If we get our self-worth from God, then why do we care what others think about us? It can become a dangerous trap. We can be pushed into sin by fearing others. Fearing man is the opposite of fearing God. Worrying about pleasing man and not God can get us into some compromising situations. Instead of measuring our lives by scripture, we become more concerned about popular opinion. Does anyone else's opinion matter? Is it worth anything? I would say not in God's eyes. We are living our lives for God, not for man. Be confident in God's word and Trust Him to take care of you.

In your soul...fear not.

image: Freepik.com

So, we can say with confidence,
"The Lord is my helper, so, I will have no fear.
What can mere people do to me?"

Hebrews 13:6

———

Can you say with confidence that the lord is your helper, and you have no fear? *Faith* is simply maintaining confidence in everything God says to us. It is believing that His words are true. It is trusting that God will honor all His promises to us. Through God's Word, we are continuously being assured that our Lord goes before us and leads us on the path we should go. God's word can never be broken.

In your soul…fear not.

When you go through deep waters, I will be with you.
When you go through rivers of difficulty,
you will not drown.
When you walk through the fire of oppression,
you will not be burned up.
The flames will not consume you.

Isaiah 43:2

Do you ever feel like you are barely keeping your head above water? Let me tell you something. You are not alone. Too many times we try so hard on our own to navigate through the rough waters. God has His hand outreached to us and is saying "Let me help you my child" and "take my hand." Many times, we don't even see His goodness because we are so clouded by our own will to do things. Let me ask you, "how is that working for you?" I suspect it's not going very well. Whatever you are going through let God be God.

In your soul...take His hand.

Trust Him

Let me hear of your unfailing love each morning,
for I trust you.
Show me where to walk, for I give myself to you.

Psalm 143:8

───

Have you had moments in your life when you feel so desperate for gods' guidance even a mere word to give you some sort of peace? Silence can often feel very lonely. That is not how many of us want to feel but we certainly experience loneliness many times Throughout our lives. God says, "I will never leave you nor forsake you." His words of encouragement fill our heart with peace. Today, be still and know that He God. He is always with you.

In your soul...rest in His presence.

Every child of God defeats this evil world, and we achieve this victory through our faith.

1 John 5:4

———

Faith in God is all we have to hold onto. It's the one truth of this life we can be assured of. Everything else is fleeting. You are a child of god; therefore, He protects you from evil. Does that mean that we will never encounter evil, no it doesn't. What it means is that we have a loving father who will shelter us from the storm. He is a hedge of protection from our enemies and a shield from their weapons. If you are under attack, run to the lord, as fast as you can, He will protect His children.

In your soul...have faith.

Those who live in the shelter of the Most High will find rest in
the shadow of the Almighty.
This I declare about the Lord:
He alone is my refuge, my place of safety.
He is my God, and I trust him.

Psalm 91:1-2

———

What is rest? Rest is when we recenter, rejuvenate, and recuperate our bodies with sleep or closing our eyes. Meditating on quiet thoughts of the day. Do we ever get enough rest? Are you in a constant state of hurriedness and worry to get everything and everyone taken care of? As busy moms we can spend every last drop of energy we have on other people, places, and things. Do we ever truly rest in the magnificence of God's grace? God gives us divine rest in Him. We can trust and rely on Him to handle our situations if we just ask. Trust He will.

In your soul...rest in the shadow of the almighty.

For we live by believing and not by seeing.

2 Corinthians 5:7

———

Has anyone ever told you a story about something that happened to them, and you just have a hard time believing them? Their story seems way too impossible to believe or to be true. Then something similar to their story happens to you. You think back, maybe they were telling the truth. Why do we always have to have something tangible, something we can touch or see for our own eyes for it to be real? Through others and our own experiences, we can say without a doubt God is real. He is found in our hearts with real evidence of His love. His spirit moves within us. Stirring up His beauty within.

In your soul...live in belief.

But when you ask him, be sure that your faith is in God alone.
Do not waiver, for a person with divided loyalty is as unsettled
as a wave of the sea that is blown and tossed by the wind.

James 1:6

———

Trust and faith go hand and hand when it comes to our beliefs in God. Praying in faith is having faith in God. Praying with faith is the prayer of the person who is completely convinced of the presence, love, power, knowledge, mercy, grace, and faithfulness of God. When you pray do you genuinely believe that God hears you and that He will take care of you? Do you struggle with trying to fix everything yourself even after you ask Him to help you? Believe Him with no doubt in your heart because, without trust in Him, we become weary of being tossed around like the wind. Trust His timing. Trust His methods. Trust His answers. Trust His heart. Trust and have faith in God and completely depend on Him.

In your soul...revel in the comfort of God's faithfulness.

Commit your actions to the Lord,
and your plans will succeed.

Proverbs 16:3

———

Today, we get so wrapped up in the behavior of others that we miss out on our blessings from God. It takes a conscious effort on our part to stop all the negative and critical feelings we have towards others. Our mouths can get us in a lot of trouble. Remember words can never be taken back no matter how many times we say sorry. Let us be intentional every day and stop the negative thoughts towards others and ourselves. Let your actions reflect God's love and grace. Also, remember we never know what someone is going through.

In your soul...be kind.

Trust in the Lord with all your heart; do not depend on your understanding. Seek his will in all you do, and he will show you which path to take.

Proverbs 3:5-6

⌒

The meaning of the word trust is a firm belief in the reliability, truth, ability, or strength of someone. That someone is God and God alone. We should have complete trust in Him, no doubts whatsoever. This scripture tells us that we should never go on our understanding because we have no idea what God's plans are for us. Scripture gives us clear instructions on how we are to trust God with everything. Mark 11:23-24 says when we seek God, and He answers our prayers it is of utmost importance that we believe Him. We are to seek Him in all we do. He has never failed us yet and...He won't.

In your soul...trust Him.

You will keep in perfect peace
all who trust in you, all whose thoughts are fixed on you.

Isaiah 26:3

———

In this scripture, God is offering us perfect peace. He wants us to keep our eyes and hearts on Him and to have unwavering trust in Him. The word "Shalom" means to be well, happy, friendly, prosperous, and healthy. It means to be whole or complete. Think about the times you are at home all by yourself, with no husband, children, friends, or in-laws. The peacefulness of the quiet warms your soul and refreshes your body. You breathe in and breathe out. Perfect peace is complete peace and guaranteed when we keep our focus on Jesus. Stay the course and stay focused. When we trust God, it shows in our actions, but it begins in our minds. Be intentional and trust God.

In your soul...embrace the blessing of perfect peace.

Those who know your name trust in you, for you, O Lord, do not abandon those who search for you.

Psalm 9:10

———

In this Scripture, David is praising God for His power over His enemies and His constant presence with Him during the battle. The deepest level of worship is praising God. Regardless of the pain, thank God for your trials and tribulations. Trusting Him when we are tempted to lose hope and loving Him. At times it can seem like God is so far away and distant from us. He never leaves us. We must rise and be strong. Always remind yourself of these things:

At my darkest, God is light.

At my weakest, God is my strength.

At my saddest, God is my comforter.

At my lowest, God is my *hope*.

In your soul...worship Him.

If our hearts do not condemn us, we have confidence before
God. We receive from him anything we ask because we keep his
commands and do what pleases him.

I John 3:21-22

—

Our hearts can deceive us, don't you think? Our hearts are connected to our feelings and sometimes our feelings and emotions cause us to stray or flounder. God has given us a conscience to both convict us and confirm us when we obey. When we make the right decisions and are obedient to God, we align ourselves with God's will for our lives. Our conscience will confirm we are on the right path. Being obedient to God's word can give us great power in our prayers. This scripture speaks of God's love for us...for you. He wants our hearts to be reassured by the power of our prayers. God has always intended for us to live a spirit-filled life and that life begins with Him. God abides in us, and we abide in Him. Which means we accept or act following His will.

In your soul...pray.

Keep me safe, O God, for I have come to you for refuge.

Psalm 16:1

———

As a small child, who do we run to when we are scared or uncertain? Who did you run to for shelter when it was raining and storming, lightning, and thunder that would shake the house? Some of us had loving parents who would hold us and tell us it was going to be okay. Or would say the thunder was not anything to fear. That it was the angels in heaven bowling. Some of us did not have such loving arms to run to or anyone who would comfort us in our time of need. But we have a loving God who wants us to come to Him in a childlike way so He can be our ultimate comforter. Our shelter. Our refuge. Our safe place. In Him, we can experience the fullness of joy. In life, our ultimate rest is in God's protective presence. Sit in that for a moment. Let the peace of knowing God is your protector and His arms are always open wide for you to rest in and feel safe.

In your soul...let Him protect you.

Not that I was ever in need, for I have learned how to be content with whatever I have.

Philippians 4:11

⁓

Are we ever truly content with life or living humbly as God would want us to? In most situations not. Give yourself some grace. Contentment is not automatic, nor does it come naturally. It is a learned skill. Only a close and intimate relationship with God can give us confidence in Him being all-sufficient. He is all we need to be content and joyful. Putting our trust in God gives us the ability to be independent of our circumstances and helps us to keep our focus on Him. The world says the meaning of contentment is the "state of being happy and satisfied." As Christians, we know that contentment can only come when we pursue a personal relationship with Christ, Himself alone, which is where we become fully satisfied.

In your soul...be content.

But I trust in your unfailing love.
I will rejoice because you have rescued me.
I will sing to the Lord because he is good to me.

Psalm 13:5-6

Have you ever heard the saying "Sing your little heart out?" It means to sing with passion and enthusiasm. When we are children, we have no inhibitions to sing loudly and with huge conviction. We do not care how we sound. We just want to be heard. Our nature is to sing with emotion and to express ourselves through the words of a song. God loves us in unexplained difficult circumstances just as much as in times of safety. Jesus died on the cross for our sins. This proves the Father's love for us and that it is unfailing. He will never fail us...ever. Trust in Him knowing that your salvation is secure and everlasting. Lean in on His truth. Sing a song of praise no matter what is going on around you. Show God love for His goodness. Let your heart and mouth rejoice...for He is your Savior.

In your soul...rejoice with gratitude.

"You don't have enough faith," Jesus told them. "I tell you the truth, if you had faith even as small as a mustard seed, you could say to this mountain, 'Move from here to there,' and it would move. Nothing would be impossible".

Matthew 17:20

———

Mustard seeds are extremely small. They grow into beautiful mustard seed shrubs. Once a shrub is grown all its parts can be eaten. Including the leaves, seeds, roots, and flowers. In this scripture, the mustard seed represents the potential of faith we can have if we just believe. As a new believer, we begin the journey with a small little mustard seed of faith. As we grow, we begin to learn about how much God loves us, that He wants to help us, and that He is always with us. When we believe in God, have faith and trust in Him. This faith that started exceedingly small becomes huge. Putting our trust and faith in God is what He asks of us. How gracious is our Father who only asks us to have a tiny little speck of faith and then, in turn, rewards us by moving mountains?

In your soul…have faith.

Let your unfailing love surround us,
Lord, for our hope is in you alone.

Psalm 33:22

———

The definition of hope is a feeling of expectation and desire for a certain thing to happen. A feeling of trust. We put hope in so many things in life. Such as we hope for more money, a better car, a bigger house, and more vacations. When don't we get these "hopes" what happens to our thoughts? Do we stay in a state of hope, or does it become hopelessness? Do things give us peace of mind? For a minute, but they are fleeting. As humans, we are never satisfied. Nothing is ever enough; we hope for more. We are empty. But when we put our hope in God, that is when our lives change and are lasting. The peace of hope in Christ gives us a level of security and strength that we never knew. Let God's unfailing love surround you and embody you in everything you do and hope for.

In your soul…live for true hope.

Trust Him

I tell you the truth, you can say to this mountain,
'May you be lifted and thrown into the sea,' and it will happen.
But you must believe it will happen and have no doubt in your
heart.

Mark 11:23

———

Having faith means trusting God even when it does not make sense. Look up. Show your face with intention. Have no doubts in your mind or heart. This scripture says you must believe! The mountain symbolizes praying with uplifted thoughts, with your mind fixed on God, above anyone or anything here on earth. God is working for you today and every day, every second, every minute, and every moment. Heaven is having conversations about you. Angels are being placed with you, to protect you. Remind your heart that God knows you are trying. God knows you are tired. Always, put Him first. Trust what He says to you through His word. His truth will set you free. He will make a better way for you even when it seems like there is no way. Have no doubts when it comes to God. Be still and know that He is GOD.

In your soul…have unwavering trust in God.

He alone is my rock and my salvation, my fortress where I will not be shaken.

Psalm 62:6

⁓

Have you ever felt so passionate about something and believed in it so much your heart hurt? I can only imagine how David's heart felt in this scripture. After enduring so many trials and tribulations in his thoughts and circumstances, he is at peace. In his heart, he truly knows God is his rock and salvation. God is his fortress. His protection against all that is evil and wants to harm him. During this time David is overwhelmed as the world tries to swallow him up. His strongholds are not of the world but his will makes God's Word and promises to never leave him His. His head reminds his heart to press on and endure. He believes God is who He says He is. His protector. His Father. His creator. Everything good. Be David. Have his heart for God. Let God be your rock and salvation. Let God be your fortress. Do not be shaken.

In your soul...stand firm in knowing God.

Trust

in THE
Lord

I remain confident of this:
I will see the goodness of the Lord in the land of the living.

Psalm 27:13

———

With all the chaos and noise that surrounds us, it can be difficult to see the goodness of God. He is constantly working things out for our good. He always has a better way. In this scripture, David talks about seeing past all the moments of despair and believing in the goodness of God. David is asking God for His continual presence, divine guidance, and protection. It takes patience on our part. Wait on the Lord. Be courageous and allow Him to give you strength through everything that may come your way. Rejoice in His goodness and will for your life. In his suffering, David calls out to God, pleading with Him to stay nearby. Are you suffering today? If you are, cry out to God, He desires to be your healer. He will stay near to you. Your God is mighty to save you. There is hope in the Lord. He is a lion. Hear Him roar against your enemies. He asks you to stand firm in faith, be confident in Him, do not run from the wicked. Wait for Him, be strong, and tell your heart to be courageous.

In your soul...embrace the goodness of God.

*And now, dear children, remain in fellowship with Christ so
that when he returns, you will be full of courage and not shrink
back from him in shame.*

1 John 2:28

⁓

Just like in the Garden of Eden when Adam and Eve sinned, they hid from God in shame. They had disobeyed Him. Do you think God wants you to feel guilt or shame for your sins? No, He wants you to acknowledge them, ask for forgiveness, and repent of them with a pure heart. There is no question about it. Christ will come back for us. This scripture emphasizes abiding in Christ. This means allowing His word to fill your mind, directing your will towards Him, and loving Him. Abiding in love means continuing to believe in His love for you. Everything God does for us is out of His abiding love for us. He wants a relationship with us. One that is pure and fulfilling, not based on shame or guilt. One on unconditional acceptance...Agape love that only He can give us. Stand firm and be confident. Be courageous for that day of reckoning will come. Stay alert and be prepared. He will take you and protect you from the evils of this world. You will be with Him for eternity.

In your soul...choose Christ.

Do not envy violent people or copy their ways.
Such wicked people are detestable to the Lord, but he offers his
friendship to the godly.

Proverbs 3:31-32

When you were young, you may have had that one friend that your parents just did not like or want you to be around. This friend was always getting into trouble and doing the wrong thing. Your parents did not want you to get yourself into any trouble or feel pressured to do something out of your character just to fit in. Your parents truly just wanted the best for you. They were trying to teach you about making the right decisions for you. This scripture says not to be jealous of evildoers and to certainly not behave in the same way. God wants the best for you, and He always will. The way of the wicked may appear easy and prosperous, but disaster always waits at the end of the road for them. It is far better to follow the road that God leads us on because this leads to endless blessings. Trust that He knows what is best for you. He will never lead you astray.

In your soul...accept God's friendship.

Trust Him

But the scriptures declare that we are all prisoners of sin, so we receive God's promise of freedom only by believing in Jesus Christ.

Galatians 3:22

⁓

Every year on the fourth of July, Americans celebrate the passage of the Declaration of Independence by the Continental Congress. Which passed on July 4, 1776. It is a celebration of *freedom*. Freedom from Great Britain, who had control of the 13 United States colonies. Each year family and friends celebrate this holiday by having backyard barbeques, grilling hamburgers and hot dogs, live music, and elaborate firework displays. The 4th of July celebration is as American as you can get. But there are no promises that the United States of America will always be free. Anything can happen at any time to change that. This scripture speaks of freedom in Christ. It speaks to your heart. To your very soul. You are sinful. We all are because of the fall of Adam and Eve in the Garden of Eden. You will never be able to keep God's law perfectly. You cannot escape your sins. But hold on, there is hope. Your hope must be in Jesus. If you genuinely believe in Christ, it is by faith that His promise is yours forever. The promise that God forgives, and we are released from sin by the blood of Jesus Christ. There is power in the cross and there is power in the blood He shed for you.

In your soul...have faith in His promises.

Whenever i am afraid,
i **trust** in *you*.

Psalm 56:3

It was by faith that even Sarah was able to have a child,
though she was barren and was too old. She believed that God
would keep his promise.

Hebrews 11:11

———

Have you ever been promised something by someone, and the promise was never kept? This person promised you that they were a safe place. Someone you could trust with everything. Even your deepest darkest secrets of shame. The heartache and disappointment can sometimes be debilitating when those promises are not kept. Broken promises can shatter all around you causing you to build up walls. Your trust in that person is gone. This scripture tells that by faith Sarah received the power to conceive, even when she was way past the age of childbearing. She stayed focused on the assurance of God's promises. Even when she knew the odds of her becoming pregnant were 0 percent, she trusted God of His word. God kept His promise and gave her and Abraham a child, named Isaac. God always keeps His promises. You will never have to have walls up or be afraid to trust God. He will never fail you.

In your soul...have faith in God's promises.

It does not rejoice about injustice but rejoices whenever the truth wins out.
Love never gives up, never loses faith, is always hopeful, and endures through every circumstance.

1 Corinthians 13:6-7

———

The true nature of man is the total opposite of the godly nature of Jesus Christ. God requires all His children to die to self and live for Christ. What does "die to self" mean? Dying to self is found in the New Testament. It means dying to your desires and trusting that God knows what is best for you. The true essence of becoming a Christian is taking up your cross and following Him every day. With intentionality, your old self dies, and you become brand new in Christ. As you grow in the fruits of the spirit, you blossom and mature by keeping your eyes on God. Let your heart submit to the spirit and humbly kneel before God asking Him to do His will in your life. This scripture teaches that God's agape love for you never gives up, never fails you, is always hopeful, and endures through any circumstances. Nothing is too big for God. He is always bigger. Love rejoices in truth.

In your soul...rejoice in His truth.

Let me ask you a question. Are you tired? Do you feel abandoned? Every word in this book is a word of God. He wants to speak to your heart. He longs for a deep soul connection with you. No matter where you are in life. No matter what you have done. God is always with you. Cling to Him. Let His words comfort you. It may feel uncomfortable to you, but that is okay. Try to sit in it. Sit in His light and rebuke the darkness. Stay awhile. Let the words truly resonate with your heart. Be brave! Jesus was sent here to save us and wash away our sins. Jesus is your mighty God. Let Him love you and show you who He is.

God is love.
God is hope.
God is peace.
God is everything good.

In your soul...trust Him with everything in you.

Milton Keynes UK
Ingram Content Group UK Ltd.
UKHW020726050424
440683UK00014B/486

9 798893 330366